D1567117

You Are a Girl

The Bible Tells Me So Press

You Are a Girl

A children's book produced by
The Bible Tells Me So Press

PUBLISHED BY
THE BIBLE TELLS ME SO CORPORATION
2111 W. CRESCENT AVE, SUITE C, ANAHEIM, CA 92801
WWW.THEBIBLETELLSMESO.COM

First Printing June, 2019

You
are
a
girl,

and we're glad to say

God made
you a girl;

He made you
that way.

As God made every part,

each toe,

a wonderful girl.

and
awesomely
made.

When
God
finished
you,

His
skill
was
displayed.

Yes, you are a girl.

It's clear as can be.

So all of your life,

There's no muddle, mistake, no mix-up, no whirl.

a beautiful
girl!

For it was You who formed
my inward parts;
You wove me together in my
mother's womb.
I will praise You, for I am awesomely
and wonderfully made;
Your works are wonderful,
And my soul knows it well.

Psalm 139:13-14

For more
books, videos, songs, and crafts
visit us online at
TheBibleTellsMeSo.com

Standing on the Bible and growing!

Made in the USA
Lexington, KY
07 November 2019